# Playing Through
**(Pronounced Thruff)**

# the Rough
**(Pronounced Ruff)**

An Irrelevant History of Golf(e), Sort Of

OR

Scotland, Shakespeare, and Golf(e)

by James B. Cash
Illustrated by Walt Kaye

D1590551

*Carney, Cole Publishing Company*
*P.O. Box 262691*
*Kettering, Ohio 45429-2691*

Library of Congress Catalog Card Number 00-133231

Printed in the United States of America

First printing
10   9   8   7   6   5   4   3   2

Additional copies of Playing Through the Rough or other publications by
James B. Cash may be ordered directly from:

**Customer Service Department
Carney, Cole Publishing Company
P.O. Box 292691
Kettering, Ohio 45429-2691**

**Cover Design and Illustrations by Walter Kaye
Layout and prepress services by Cam-Tech Publishing**

*Humor, Golf,  Scotland,  British History*

**ISBN 0-925436-20-8**

Also by James B. Cash

*Unsung Heroes: Ohioans in the White House: A Modern Appraisal*

*ISBN: 1-882203-22-4*                    *1998*

Also illustrated by Walt Kaye

*His Only Hope ... A Child's View Of Organ Donation*

*1998*

*To My Parents*

*Frank Ernest Cash and Mary Burris Cash*

*Educators and Golfers*

# Table of Contents

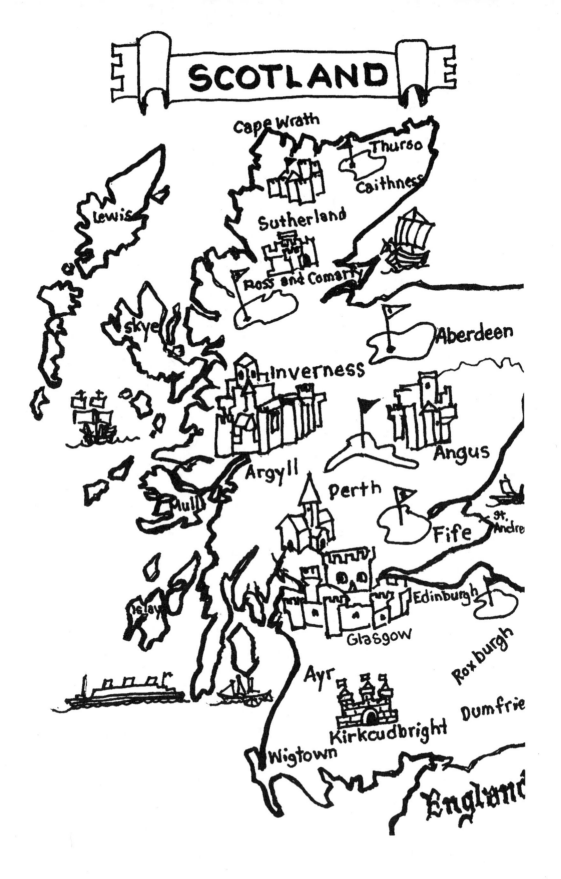

# Preamble

## I. Genesis

It was a dark and stormy night...

The thunder rolled, great sheets of rain splashed onto the dampened earth, the wind, whistling through the trees, lashed out at the land when suddenly out of the cacophony came a stentorian voice with a slightly Scottish burr:

## Let There Be Golf!

Nothing happened ...

The Stentorian voice spoke out again:

I said, **LET THERE BE GOLF!**

Still, nothing happened ...

The voice cleared its stentorian throat

In mid-clear, a smaller but just as authorative voice said:

**Wait, the Infrastucture's Not There.**

The original voice said: **Huh? Oh!**

# Let There Be Golf!

*It was a dark and stormy night ...*

The infrastructure took a while to get going.

It started with natural forces.

*It started with natural forces ...*

There was linksand, water, wind, grass, gorse, with perhaps a burn cutting across the grass to the sea. The winds and water sculpt the linksand. Grass encroaches where it can. Seabirds came ashore to eat. They fertilize the grass. Sheep or other grazing animals keep the grass under control. Rough plants like gorse and heather provide boundaries. This is all in a place that became known as Scotland. It is the perfect environment for golfe.

The rest is up to people. They came. Many types from all directions: Stone Age People, Kelts, Picts, Brits, Angles, Germans, Romans.

*People came to Pre-Scotland from all directions*

# JJ. Roman Roamin'

As with many basic things the Romans got involved. In 55 B. C. Julius Caesar invaded Britain-to-be. The Romans brought a game called paganica (village game) played with a feather stuffed ball (pila). This game was observed by Caledonian witches. They thought it might be the basis for a pretty good international game, except Witch 1 decided that the game was too easy, and that "the players were too happy". It would require "further development". The other witches thought that she was being too "Picty".

While in Britain-to-be, Caesar acquired a taste for pre-Angus beef, about which he made one of his least famous statements *I came, I saw, I ate*. This was to lead to Caesar's downfall after he returned to Rome. While he was out casting dice at a Rubicon casino, some pasta makers complained to a senate subcommittee about his imports of beef. Cassius (who had a lean and hungry look) reflected this in his famous speech pitching for pasta funds: *Upon what meat does this our Caesar feed that he has grown so great?* (Emphasis added).

Things went downhill from then on, and on 15 March (Ides) 44 B. C. Caesar was assassinated by members of the senate, including Brutus *the noblest Roman of them all*. Caesar, always a shrewd observer, noticed that Brutus was in on it said, *Et tu Brute? Then Caesar falls.*

*Caesar was always a shrewd observer*

Two years later, the senate with pangs of guilt voted to name the hottest month of the year for Caesar. The fireworks and Roman candle lobby also advocated a holiday "around the fourth" for celebration, but this was snuffed. Later Caesar Augustus successfully lobbied for a month named August by promising a few roads and aqueducts to senators.

The northern part of Britain-to be was called Caledonia by the Romans. In 81 A. D. General Gnaeus Agricola invaded the area. He pushed "agricola culture" as an alternative to continuous fighting. This didn't work and in 122 A. D. Roman leader Hadrian had a wall built in southern Caledonia to keep the Picts in. The wall would later be used as a hazard for early golfe courses.

*Roman General Agicola encouraged "Agricola culture"*

# III. It May Have Started With Witches

There were three witches on a heath:

Witch 1.
> *Boil, Boil toil and bubble,*
> *Eye of Newt make it trouble.*
> *Warm spit and grapefruit rind,*
> *What has't thee done to bedevil mankind?*

*The three witches who invented golf(e)*

Witch 2.

> *I'l invent something complex and arcane,*
> *That every spring people will pray for rain,*
> *To wash away records and facts,*
> *I'l call my invention an income tax.*

Witch 3.

> *Bigger plans I'l have my say,*
> *Many a multilane highway,*
> *When one gets going like the wind,*
> *They'l have to stop for fender bend.*

Witch 1 chuckled at the earnestness of Witch 2 and 3. They were young and they meant badly, but they just didn't have the scope, the intensity, the grand vision. She presented her own plan:

> *A game I'l invent with a little white ball,*
> *Hit toward a flag or off a wall,*
> *Bunkers and divots and sand traps too,*
> *People will play and cuss like blue.*
> *I'l gie them a long shot or occasional putt,*
> *People will lie and yearn for smut.*

Witches 2 and 3 stood in awe.

> *We'l call it golfe when it is done,*
> *No one will forget, no one. None.*

Witch 1 ahgh (clearing her throat). Projecting louder-

> *When shall we three meet again*
> *In thunder, lightning, or in rain?*

(Witch 1 was much better at inventing bedeviling games than scheduling).

Witch 2

> *When the hurlyburly's done,*
> *When the battle's lost and won.*

Witch 3.

> *That will be ere the set of sun.*

14

Witch 1.
   *Where the place?*
Witch 2.
   *Upon the heath.*
Witch 3.
   *There to meet with Macbeth.*
Witch 1.
   *I come, Graymalkin!*
Witch 2
   *Paddock calls.*
Witch 3
   *Anon!*

All. (Starting to specify some of the rules).
   *Fair is foul, and foul is fair:*
   *Hover through the fog and filthy air.*

They vanish.

(In the background weakly and mysteriously)—

   *You say call it golfe?*

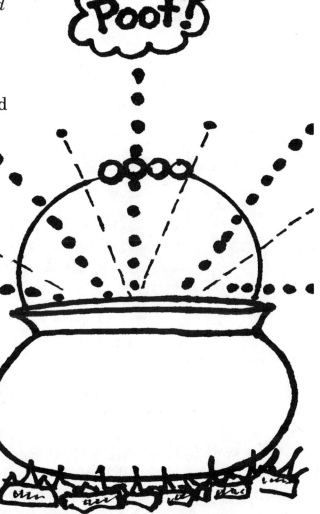

*The witches disappear*

*Rabbit observing
the first golf(e) shot*

One day in the summer of 999 a bored shepherd hit a stone into a rabbit hole. His bored sheepdog retrieved it. The dog told his friends about their new game, and soon bored shepherds all over the land were hitting stones into holes. Cussing was invented. The wool industry declined.

*Two shepherds arguing about type
and quality of rock used for golf(e)*

The next year to celebrate Y1K there was a tournament for shepherds. Someone brought liquid, fermented corn. There was a fight about the type and quality of rocks used for the game, and their marking. The winning shepherd's name is unknown to history. Only the sheepdogs know.

# AMBLE

## I. Macbeth and Golfe

### A. Our Links to Simpler Times

The first known foursome consisted of a king, two generals, and a nobleman. The course was simple and circular with fourteen "wholes" towards a centre field of parsnips. If one hit the parsnips within the allotted number of "strokes" one could be said to be playing "at parsnips".

The king, Duncan, was a very steady player. He was not strong, but always hit it forward, usually playing parsnips golf. Macbeth, the biggest hitter in Scotland, could hit the ball "a Scottish mile", but he had a wicked slice. Under Duncan's rules he was penalized for this because it wouldn't always stay in the right fairway. He would have to hit it back to the correct fairway before he could go for the parsnips.

Another of Duncan's rules was that when hitting towards others on the course the golfer would have to yell, *Watch out those that are going before!* Macbeth thought that was easy for a dribbler like Duncan to say. If he hit someone it wouldn't hurt any way. Besides Macbeth thought yelling interfered with his follow-through (pronounced follow-thruff in those days). Any way Duncan's rules got on Macbeth's

**WATCH OUT THOSE THAT ARE GOING BEFORE!**

*The first warning in golf(e)*

*Macbeth seethed under Duncan's rules*

17

nerves causing him to seethe.

The third player, Banquo was a pale imitation of Macbeth. He tagged along behind Macbeth to the wrong fairways and back. He didn't have a ghost of a chance. Finally there was Macduff, the worst golfer of them all. He might hit it anywhere within a 360 degree angle. He hit walls, bunkers, and sheep. One time after missing a forward shot while bringing his club back, he knocked the ball backward with much more than normal force. He tried a backward stance, but couldn't hit it consistently. Of course his name has been immortalised for all time by a type of player known as a Macduffer.

*Macduff hit the ball backwards, giving a nickname to a type of golfer*

There were some other problems. In the summer parts of Scotland have 20 hours of daylight. Duncan was a morning person. He got up and called upon Macbeth before the first cock would crow. Macbeth would- *Get up at night and dress by yellow candlelight*. This caused some problems at home. Lady Macbeth was a light sleeper and the candlelight always disturbed her. Further, she didn't under-stand or like golfe anyway. They had a long argument. She thought he ought to stay home and work around the castle, helping them qualify for the Designer Castle of the Year 1040.

*Macbeth got up by candlelight and disturbed Lady Macbeth*

*An errant Macduff shot headed for Birnham Woods*

He explained to her that he couldn't turn down a game with the King. She got the final words in though:

*...Come you spirits*
*That tend on mortal thoughts, unsex me here;*
*And fill me from the crown to the toe topfull !*

*Of direst cruelty!  Make thick my blood,*
*Stop up the access and passage to remorse,*
*That no compunctious visitings of nature*
*Shake my fell purpose nor keep peace between*
*The effect and it!*

She went on.  Macbeth pretty well tuned her out.  But what was this about "unsex me"?  Does this mean even more headaches? sleepwalking?  He couldn't help but notice all the exclamation points.  He concluded that she was just being dramatic.

One day, both foul and fair, they were playing their usual game: Duncan dribbling the ball forward towards the parsnips, Macbeth slicing off the fairway with Banquo following, and Macduff firing off into Birnham woods.

*Damn, if the woods had only been closer to the castle!*

Macbeth was particularly feeling the pressure.

*Does he think us such simple fools?*
*To blindly accept such stupid rules!*

They were in the second round.  Duncan was at parsnips, Macbeth with some excellent, if misdirected strokes, was three over, Banquo was a little behind, and Macduff was still finishing the first round.

Banquo remarked, *I wonder if he was born of woman?*  The three-some snickered.

On the thirteenth whole in the heath area, Macbeth and Banquo encountered the witches.  They greeted Macbeth as Thane of Glamis, (his then approved thaneship) Thane of Cawdor, and future King. Macbeth didn't give it too much thought.  They told Banquo that his descendants would be kings.  Now *Macbeth* had always been sceptical about the accuracy of witches' reports, finding them only a little more credible than playwrights or traveling "journalists".  When they caught up with the king at the parsnips, Duncan surprised them by saying to Macbeth, *I am naming thee Thane of Cawdor.*  He then said he planned to visit their castle, *within a fortnight.*

When Macbeth told Lady Macbeth, she liked the additional thaneship. That might entitle her, them, to another 1/2 servant FTE, probably half a Harold or half a Jack or at least half a page. The kingship? She smiled her crooked little smile. But the visit to the castle caused her panic. No way a Thane and Thanette, even double ones, could get the castle ready on such short notice. They didn't even have a king-sized bed. What was Duncan up to anyway?

Macbeth thought about becoming king. He could establish his own golfe rules. No more narrow fairways. They would be widened out for heavy hitters. He could simplify the warning. And why not 18 wholes? Also as king there would be more FTE's around the castle, Lady Mac could resex herselfe and that might help *him* relax. He might get rid of his wicked slice.

*"If chance will have me king, why, chance may crown me Without my stir."*

But how could it happen?  Maybe it would just happen.

*If chance will have me king, why, chance may crown me*
*Without my stir.*

The next game at the 19th whole (another reason Macbeth thought there should be 18 *playing wholes*.  It just wasn't logical to play 14 wholes and then go to the 19th whole.  Duncan was a nice guy.  He just wasn't logical .  After the winner, Duncan, of course, bought a round for all, he asked his son and cadet, Malcolm for a report on the previous Thane of Cawdor:

Malcolm said he died pretty well:

*Nothing in his life*
*Became him like the leaving it; he died*
*As one that had been studied in his death*
*To throw away the dearest thing he ow'd*
*As ' twere a careless trifle.*

They drank another round for the late Thane.  Then the sanguine Duncan announced that he was going to make Malcolm the Prince of Cumberland!  This was a blow.  Malcolm a cadet who'd learned golfe at his father's side!  If he became king there was no hope for the game.  Macbeth mumbled into his cup:

*The Prince of Cumberland!-That is a step,*
*On which I must fall down or else o'er leap,*
*For in my way it lies.  Stars hide your fires!*
*Let not light see my deep and black desires:*
*The eye wink at the hand! yet let that be,*
*Which the eye fears, when it is done to see.*

At the castle Duncan and Macbeth discussed potential rule changes.  Duncan listened patiently, but was adamant.  He explained the new Prince of Cumberland (former golfe cadet, Malcom) had learned the game from him, and it would be unfair to change the rules at this time.  Macbeth thought *damn, a dribbling game of fourteen wholes into the next generation.  Who would save golfe?  He knew he had to act.*  He concluded:

*I have no spur*
*To prick the sides of my intent, but only*

*Vaulting ambition which o'erleaps itself,*
*And falls on the other.*

On the other hand, he was feeling a little ambivalent.  He told Lady Macbeth he rather enjoyed:

*Golden opinions from all sorts of people,*
*Which would be worn now in their newest gloss,*
*Not cast aside so soon.*

She bucked him up:

*Art thou afeared*
*To be the same in thine own act and valour*
*As thou art in desire?*

He answered:

*Pr'ythee, peace*
*I dare do all that may become a man;*
*Who dares do more is none.*

He raised a few more points, but her arguments prevailed.  He concluded:

*I am settled, and bend up*
*Each corporal agent to this terrible feat.*
*Away and mark the time with fairest show:*
*False face must hide what false heart must know.*

Anyway Duncan was murdered in his sleep in the new king-sized bed.  But Macbeth didn't feel so good.  He described his feelings in great detail:

*Me thought I heard a voice cry,*
*Sleep no more!*
*Macbeth does murder sleep,-the innocent sleep;*
*Sleep that knits up the ravell'd sleeve of care,*
*The death of each day's life, sore labour's bath,*
*Balm of hurt minds, great nature's second course,*
*Chief nourisher in life's feast.*

and,

*Whence is that knocking?*
*How is't with me, when every noise appals me?*
*What hands are here? Ha they pluck out mine eyes!*
*Will all great Neptune's ocean wash this blood*
*Clean from my hand? No; this my hand will rather*
*The multitudinous seas incarnadine*
*Making the green one red.*

and,

*Had I but died an hour before this chance,*
*I had liv'd a blessed time; for, from this instant,*
*There's nothing serious in mortality:*
*All is but toys: renown and grace is dead;*
*The wine of life is drawn, and the mere lees*
*Is left this vault to brag of.*

Lady Macbeth had
heard enough of this
negative thinking.
She also noticed some
anti-social behaviour:

*How now my lord! why*
*do you keep alone,*
*Of sorrowist fancies*
*your companions mak-*
*ing;*
*Using those thoughts*
*which should indeed*
*have died*
*With them they think*
*on? Things without all*
*remedy*
*Should be without*
*regard: What's done is*
*done.*

Macbeth pointed out
that Duncan may be

*Lady Macbeth was resolute*

better off than they are:

*...Duncan is in his grave;*
*After life's fitful fever he sleeps*
*well*
*Treason has done its worst: nor*
*steel nor poison,*
*Malice domestic, foreign levy,*
*nothing,*
*Can touch him further.*

## B. New Rules at Last!

Anyway Macbeth had a chance to
make the rules for golfe and
Lady Macbeth got her extra help
to begin a castle renovation program.  He changed the course
from circular to sequential.  He
widened the fairways, and established the out and back system so
they would always end up at the

*Macbeth gets to write new sensible*
*golf(e) rules, while Lady Macbeth gets*
*to redecorate Dunsinane*

clubhouse.  He also sought to established 18 wholes as standard, but
there was a parsnip shortage.  Macbeth put Scotland on an emergency parsnips growing program.  Finally he shortened the warning
to, *Watch before thee.*  After he was done he made a statement to the
surrounding courtiers, jacks, heralds, pages and cadets:

*Now at last an eternal game!*
*To it forever I'l owe my fame.*

But Banquo was a worry.  Well really not Banquo, who was a pretty
good guy if a duplicitous player.  But if his children were kings?
Fleance and his children?  Fleance hadn't shown the slightest interest in golfe.  He didn't even cadet for his father.  No-Banquo and his
descendants would have to go.

So Macbeth hired some hitmen, and to cover it up asked Lady
Macbeth and her assembled retinue to have a party for Banquo.
They even hit upon a felicitous name for the party-a Banquoit!  Well
the hitmen got Banquo, but Fleance escaped.  Macbeth thought:

*The game of golfe imperiled is,*
*Out of my hands and into*
*Fleances', his!*

Things got even worse. Banquo's ghost showed up at the Banquoit! Macbeth nearly lost it right there. Clearly it was time to check in with the witches again.

Back to the heath-

When the witches showed up they said a few verses showing how witchy they were. Macbeth said he needed some vital information. They showed off a little by bringing up some apparitions. The first apparition told him to beware Macduff. Macduff! He couldn't hit the parsnips with a bowling ball! But just in case, he decided to wipe out Macduff's family.

Another apparition arose and said:

*Be bloody, bold and resolute;*
*laugh to scorn*
*The power of man, for none of*
*woman born*
*Shall harm Macbeth!*

Well that was certainly comforting. Even further, another apparition told him he didn't have to worry:

*Macbeth shall never vanquish'd*
*be, until*
*Great Birnham wood to high*
*Dunsinane hill*

*Banquo's ghost showed up at the Banquoit*

*Shall come against him.*

Now he was getting somewhere. He had one more big question. It was about Banquo's issue, specifically Fleance and descendants. The witches did some pyrotechnics, threw a few more visions at him and disappeared.

The Macbeths got back to their favorite pastimes: Macbeth playing golfe and Lady Macbeth renovating the castle. She was especially keen on new wall hangings and a modern kind of torch. Dunsinane was a shoe-in for Designer Castle of the year. Macbeth was playing subparsnips golfe (with a new foursome). But it wasn't good enough. There was a group including Malcolm, his uncle Siward, young Siward and Macduff organizing an attack on Dunsinane. In the meanwhile Lady Macbeth was having some kind of breakdown associated with the original clean-up:

*Out, damned spot! out, I say!*
*One, two; why then tis time to do't.*
*Hell is murky! Fie, my lord, Fie!*
*a soldier and afeard?*
*What we need we fear, who knows it,*
*when none can call our power to account?*
*Yet who would have thought the old man*
*to have so much blood in him?*

*The three witches conjure up an apparition*

*Lady Macbeth has trouble with cleaning*

Macbeth built a course next to the castle.  The critic for *The Dunsinane News* predicted that this would start a hole new trend in real estate.  But Lady Macbeth was not doing well. Macbeth brought the doctor in.  The doctor prescribed a couple of swallows of frog's blood potion (FBP), and "a good night's rest."  In the meanwhile Macbeth put his armour on to face the enemy.  He was confident:

*I will not be afraid of death and bane,*
*Till Birnham forest come to*
*Dunsinane.*

The enemy cut some boughs from
Birnham wood and moved forward.
Seyton, one of Macbeth's officers said:

*The queen, my lord is dead.*

Macbeth replies:

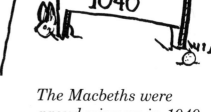

*She should have died hereafter;*
*There would have been a time for such a word.*
*To-morrow, and to-morrow, and to-morrow,*
*Creeps in this petty pace from day to day,*
*To the last syllable of recorded time;*
*And all our yesterdays have lighted fools*
*The way to dusty death. Out, out, brief*
*candle!*

*The Macbeths were*
*proud winners in 1040*

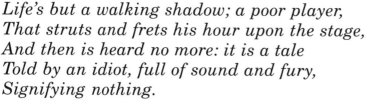

*Life's but a walking shadow; a poor player,*
*That struts and frets his hour upon the stage,*
*And then is heard no more: it is a tale*
*Told by an idiot, full of sound and fury,*
*Signifying nothing.*

Then he saw Birnham wood moving toward Dunsinane.  *Hmm,* thought Macbeth.  And then the final confrontation with Macduff. Macbeth, staying cool, told Macduff of his charmed life, quoting the witches, "*...for none born of woman shall harm Macbeth!* Macduff replied:

*Birnham Woods heads for Dusinane*

*Despair thy charm;*
*And let the angel whom thou hast serv'd*
*Tell thee, Macduff was from his mother's womb.*
*Untimely ripped.*

Macbeth knew that he was finished, but he refused to yield, breathlessly replying:

*Yet I will try the last.  Before my body*
*I throw my warlike shield: lay on Macduff;*
*And damned be him that first cries, Hold enough!*

MACBETH

1010?- 1057

LIAR, TRAITOR, MURDERER; BUT LOOK WHAT HE DID FOR GOLFE!

Macduff layed on and that took care of Macbeth.

---

As we pause to think about the story, we must concede Macbeth at times went too far. He was overzealous, leaving us a tortured legacy. Perhaps this legacy is best summed up by an anonymous golfer:

*He may have been a liar, a traitor, and a murderer, but look what he did for golf.*

Anonymous golfer

# II. Golfe Moves on~Wallace and Bruce

## A. A Note on Wales and England:

For better or for worse Scotland shared its main isle with two other nations: the small nation of Wales and the colossus England. Wales was to give the world poets, actors, singers, writers and, through America, two of the greatest names in the history of golf. In the colossus there was always something going on: in prehistory there was Stonehenge. Then around 500 A.D. a young knight pulled a sword out of a stone, which set in motion a whole series of events. Finally just after the Macbeths died, William the Conqueror and the Norman French successfully invaded England. They defeated the Anglo-Saxons and their king, Harold the Loser. The Normans were to spread around the British Isles, and ulti- mately have a great impact on golf.

*William Wallace*

*King Edward I was rumoured to have pushed potential advisor out of the window for "demonstration purposes"*

## B. Meanwhile Back to Scotland

The next innovations in golfe came from the great military leaders of Scotland: William Wallace and Robert the Bruce.

Wallace, known by some as Braveheart, was a bold and courageous leader. He fought the perpetual enemy England led by the ruthless Edward I. Edward liked to pick on little nations like Wales and Scotland. He was also rumoured to have thrown his son's best friend and advisor out of a castle tower.

Robert the Bruce was a sometime ally to Wallace and a sometime ally to Edward. When the Scottish king Alexander III died from a fall off a horse in 1286 he left only one heir, an infant half-Norwegian girl named Margaret. Edward was her great uncle. Next in line, but rather distant were John Balliol (The Empty Coat) and Robert the Bruce, both from Norman French families. Edward coveting Scotland and its great golfe courses worked out a deal to make Margaret queen. But Margaret died on her way to Scotland. Edward then picked Balliol, who agreed to let Edward and his retinue start playing the courses whenever they wanted to.

Scottish players didn't like this, however, and urged Balliol to lead a revolt. Balliol tried, but Edward sent his troops back to Scotland and easily defeated the Scots at Dunbar. He added further conditions: all greens fees would be waived for the English. The Scots regarded this as threatening their national game. This hit close to their hearts-their pocketbooks. How would they pay for maintenance? They drafted a new military leader, William Wallace. Wallace was not a king, nor one of the great chieftains, but a lesser land owner chosen because of his talent; thus to some extent he democratized war.

The next time Edward sent troops to Scotland under an assistant, John de Warenne, Wallace was ready for them with a special defence of bunkers, sandtraps, and water hazards. This along with his extraordinary "mooning" tactic (*Go'blimy, look there's nothing under those kilts!*) totally befuddled the English. The English lost at Stirling bridge in 1297 between the 13th and 14th wholes.

*The English were befuddled by mooning tactics of the Scots*

Edward, who had been in

France, got mad, threw a few people into the English Channel and headed for Scotland. He beat Wallace at Falkirk in 1298 before Wallace had a chance to prepare the course. Wallace retreated to the Highlands. There he was betrayed by a soccer ball manufacturer's representative who thought Wallace was devoting too much national effort to golfe. The English executed Wallace in 1305.

*Edward I throws a few advisors into the English Channel*

Bruce stepped in to the vacuum. He was tired of the English coming north and tearing up the courses. He fought six skirmishes with the English without achieving a great victory. He went across the "multitudinous sea incarnadine" to the original home of the Scots, Ireland, to sharpen his game and make the English think he was dead.

There he made two discoveries. First he noticed the greenness of Ireland. Clearly the game could use that kind of color. Second, the Irish were ahead of the world in golfe course maintenance. They had a special kind of sheep, the Roscommon, that ate the grass very close to the ground. Where they had eaten, one could roll the ball rather than bouncing it towards the parsnips. Eventually Bruce would adapt such golfe course maintenance technology to Scotland and, as a tribute to Ireland, call such cleared areas "greens".

While in Ireland, Bruce was placed behind a slow foursome; thus he dawdled around the clubhouse watching a spider. He watched the spider swing across some beams in the clubhouse six times without success. Bruce began to wonder: *Is that spider ever going to make it?* On the seventh try-bingo!

Many might have walked away at that point, but Bruce, knowing he could always catch up with his foursome continued to watch the spider. The spider spun its web and waited. Its victims came and were entangled in the web. He hit upon a wonderful idea. That's what he would do to the English!

*An anonymous spider gave Robert the Bruce the idea for fighting the English*

Returning home to Scotland he won a victory at Loudon Hill. When learning of Bruce's victory Edward literally had apoplexy. Before he died he made Edward II, aka "Little Eddie", promise to carry his bones until the Scots were defeated. Little Eddie who had, of course, to operate without his thrown-out-of-a-tower best friend and advisor, dropped the bones. He asked the servants to reconnect them. The servants asked for a "bone plan".

Finally he headed to Scotland with the bones still unconnected. He wasn't quite sure where to go, but the natives suggested that a place called Bannockburn would be a good place to start. Bannockburn had been well prepared with traps and bunkers

*The servants ask Little Eddie for a "bone plan"*

used to narrow the field thereby negating the English advantage in numbers. Bruce was there with his Irish spider strategy waiting for the English to entrap themselves. They did and were routed, scattering 22 battle flags among the sand traps, bunkers, and water hazards. It was one of the greatest English military defeats ever.

Bruce saw this all as a divine message, replacing the hard-to-grow parsnips with the battle flags, and establishing a 22-hole course and Scottish independence—for a while.

*Bannockburn after the battle*

# III. Five J's, a Mary, John Knox, and a Double J

## A. Five Jimmys

The French fought the English; the English alternated between fighting the French and the Scots; and the Scots alternated between fighting the English and each other. These arrangements naturally led the Scots and the French to be sometime friends.

In 1346 in a major battle the English bowmen-yeoman slaughtered French knights and barons at Crecy. This taught a lesson to the Scots that was to have its impact on golfe and futeball.

The Scots had developed a new royal family named Stewart or Stuart. The Stewarts had five Jameses in a row ($J^1$ through $J^5$), a Mary and a double James($J^6$ and $J^1$).

The first James was sent to France to escape the English. Unfortunately the English captured him and made him a prisoner-guest for 18 years. By the time he got home he had little time to develop his game.

The Scots, meanwhile, were enjoying the game. $J^2$, well aware of this, saw golfe and futeball (soccer) as threats to the national defence *i. e.* the practise of archery. Cynics also stated that he had trouble getting tee time and didn't dare pull the old English trick of royal prerogative for fear of starting another war. In 1457 he issued a decree *that futeball and golfe be utterly cryit down and nocht usit...* Strangely or perhaps not so, in 1460 when $J^2$ was out looking at new military technology- a cannon- it blew up and killed him. A witchy looking woman was reported nearby.

$J^3$ did not seem to learn much from that incident. In 1471 he renewed the ban on futeball and golfe because *futeball and golfe be abusit in tyme coming...* In 1488 the Scots again rebelled and $J^3$ was killed, reportedly by a mashie shot. The Scots played on.

During the same period the English decided to have their own Civil War- the War of the Roses between the white roses of York and the red roses of Lancaster. The Yorkists were led by the murdering, conniving Richard III ($R^3$) who offered his kingdom for a horse. He

*King James II banned golf(e) and futeball*

didn't get it and Lancaster (Henry Tudor) became Henry VII (H[7]).

MY KINGDOM FOR A HORSE!

*Richard III*

J[4] took some time out for a little wedded bliss, marrying Margaret Tudor, H[7]'s daughter, the sister of the future King Henry VIII (H[8]) of England. This was called the union of the thistle and the rose, which will become important to our story.

For golfe and futeball he issued the most severe regulation, *It is statut and ordainit that in na place of the realme there be usit futeball, golfe or other unprofitabill sportis...* Still the Scots golfed on. J[4] decided to examine first-hand the phenomenon of golfe. Thus he got the royal treasury to spring for a set of clubes and balls (stuffed with feathers and called featheries). After five-putting one of the wholes, he decided *It wae ane uncommonly stupid game...*, and he would return to his first love–war.

Inspired by a charismatic witch, he stowed away his clubes and featheries, and headed south to Northumberland and Flodden Field. He, too, met a violent end, reportedly niblicked to death.

J[5] had a minimal impact on golfe (or futeball). He met with his uncle, H[8] of England, over lunch of stag, beef, pork, mutton, and goat. H[8] thought J[5] ate like a fuzzing bird. Between the beef and the pork, H[8] suggested that if J[5] seized church land in Scotland, and in H[8]'s terms, *turned it into golfe courses, or at least driving ranges, he could do much for golfe.* J[5] seemed cautious, worrying about his reputation.

H[8] said,

*Things done well,*
*And with a care,*

*Exempt themselves from fear.*

J[5] remained reluctant.

H[8] in a way agreed,

*As Griffith once said-*
*Men's evil deeds live in brass,*
*Their virtues we write in water.*

J[5] said, *Who's Griffith?*

Anyway, J[5] returned to Scotland, to see his daughter Mary born, and to see himself die six days later. Mary would take the game of golfe to the next level.

*King Henry VIII thought James V ate like a bird*

*Henry VIII suggested that church land could be used for golf(e) courses or at least driving ranges*

# B. Mary, Queen of Scots

MQoS was an extraordinary person: pretty, witty, charming, and also had enough Tudor blood to be a good, but not enough to be a great intriguer. Mostly raised in France, Mary's French-Scottish accent caused her to pronounce *cadet* as *caddie* and thus it became.

Mary led a challenging and dramatic life. One of her greatest challenges was a man named John Knox. Knox, born a peasant, was educated to be a Catholic priest and notary, with strong educational and professional connections to St. Andrews. However, he became frustrated with the established church, and turned around and founded Presbyterianism. This was to have a dramatic impact on golfe.

Knox, a disciple of John Calvin, was a strong advocate of individual responsibility. He was impatient with hierarchies of all kinds. Of course, Mary was at the top of a hierarchy. She thought Knox ought to be deferential. They clashed on a number of things. Mary liked fancy clothes, pageantry, and fun. Knox preferred basic black, simplicity, and agony. For a while he hassled Mary about golfe. She asked him to try it. He did and was surprised. Knox immediately saw two things in golfe. It was a game of individuals out on their own, and at times it was agonizing. Thus it wasn't too bad for Presbyterians.

*Mary Queen of Scots golfing as her husband's funeral cortege passes by*

So MQoS golfed on. One day when she was on the course, she was recorded as the first and most famous person who temporarily stopped, held her hand over her heart while the funeral cortege of her spouse (Lord Darnley) passed by. She also played golfe with her cousin, Elizabeth I of England. Elizabeth, who was nine years older than Mary and wore a stiff collar, played a conservative

English style game, hitting straight forward for a lot of pars. Mary played the Celtic game of chance, finding many traps, going out of bounds, but at times, making beautiful shots. One highlight was the first birdie on the par 4, 8th whole.

Initially Mary had hooked the ball into the woods on her first shot. She was lucky to get out of the woods and into a sandtrap next to the green on her second shot. On her third shot she hit a bird and the ball ricocheted in, thus achieving the first birdie.*

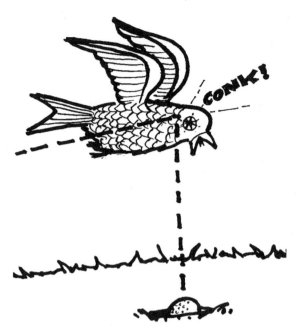

*The First Birdie*

Three things about Elizabeth got on Mary's nerves: her golfing outfit, especially the stiff collar, the conservative approach to the game, and Elizabeth's continuous talk about virginity. Mary, who had been engaged at one, and entered into her first of three marriages at 16, simply couldn't relate. Of course if Elizabeth had no heirs, Mary, who was 1/4 Tudor, would become Mary, Queen of England, $M^2QoE$, if she could keep her head. This would allow her to spread golfe through the entire isle.

_____

*This should not be confused with a much later development, *the eagle,* when an eagle picked up a ball after a second shot on a par four whole, carried it and dropped it in *for an eagle-drop.* (Of course *drop* was later dropped). See below for theories on eagle motivation.

*Queen Elizabeth at golf(e)*

42

At whole 16, Elizabeth played around a water hazard. If Mary hit it over, she would show Elizabeth how the game could be played! Kerplunk! Elizabeth not only pointed out that it would cost Mary penalty strokes, but that the English were going to establish colonies in the New World, and that one of them might be named for her condition! Mary blew up. Elizabeth told her it wasn't something to lose her head over. But she did.

In the meanwhile Knox lived on, turning the Presbyterian church into the Church of Scotland. In a church without a hierarchy, it needed discipline and rules, which the tireless Knox provided. It didn't take the canny Scots long to take the same approach to golfe.

*Mary played the Celtic game of chance*

# Theories on Eagle Motivation

Scholars have argued for years as to why an eagle picked a golf ball off a fairway, flew to the green and dropped it in (for a two on a par four hole). John Knox would have called it predestination. However, not many modern scholars argue for predestination. Today there are two basic schools of thought on the cause of the eagle: the minimalists and the maximalists. The minimalists say that it was a case of mistaken identity. They say the eagle attracted to the ball containing feathers thought it was either a strange kind of egg or a new kind of animal. Then discovering that it was neither, dropped it and it happened to go into the hole. Of course within the minimalist school there is a division of opinion and often bitter quarrels between the eggists and the animalists.

The maximalists, on the other hand, *think the eagle knew what he was doing.* But they, too, have their divisions: The universalist group says golf is aligned with universal principles of nature, and has an appeal not only for man, but for all of nature. They have documented many instances where animals have intervened in the game. The exceptionalists think that *that* eagle, and other intervening animals were exceptional- stating in their graceless language: *Ones of a kinds.* Of course they are divided between those that think the eagle was serious and others that do not. The serious school is divided between those who think the eagle wanted to demonstrate his exceptionalism, in other words, was just showing off; and others who think it was a cry of anguish reaching out to his fellow creatures. The non-serious school think the eagle was just playing a joke.

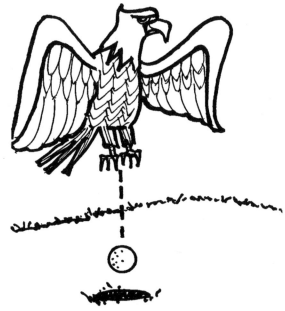

*The first eagle*

Of course there are refereed journals, annual conferences, constantly shifting alliances and rancorous debates on the entire issue. Only people of the maximalist, exceptionalist, non-serious school seem to enjoy them.

## Some Bogey Comments:

In the U. K. bogey means par. Thus the mythical Colonel Bogey plays all holes at par. There is even a famous march named after him (used in the movie *Bridge over the River Kwai).* In the U. S. a bogey is one over. Why? The explanation goes back to the origin of golf. Remember the great Scottish courses were creations of nature. A part of nature included bogs. Thus the Scots thought that getting *boggeyed doon* was normal. Americans, on the other hand, created their own courses. A bog would be a barrier on the side. Getting bogged down on an American course was regarded as exceptional. How could someone that got bogged down be said to be playing at par? Thus the difference. A *double bogey*, a U. S. term, obviously means getting out of the bog and then back in. It applies to more than golf.

# C. James VI and I. Golfe Spreads and Becomes Golf

When MQoS literally lost her head, and Elizabeth failed to produce heirs by immaculate conception, MQoS's son, $J^6$ of Scotland, became next in line for the English throne. In 1603 after Elizabeth died, an English group came north to recruit him to come down to England. The English pointed out the advantages of moving south: balmier weather, a more laid back life style, with fewer civil wars and rebellions. $J^6$ wasn't so sure. He was comfortable in Scotland. The Scottish parliament had waived his greens fees, he was playing almost every day, and he had recently lowered his handicap to 12. Besides there was a certain comfort in being the sixth James.

*King James VI and I enjoyed working on "his" Bible*

The English caucused with a Celtic witch-consultant. Clearly they would have to come up with an attractive package. When they reconvened with $J^6$, they made the point that the first five James's hadn't done all that well, and that in England he would have a clean slate, becoming James I ($J^1$). Furthermore if he wanted to remain $J^6$ of Scotland they would *interpose no objections.* Scotland could keep its own government and so could England, but for PR purposes they would call the whole thing *Great Britain!*

Like many a Scot James remained cool. The English sensed that.

They decided to unleash their last two weapons.

*There is a top secret project that we can't reveal, but it would make your name a household word.*

James looked up. *What is it?*

The delegation was cautious; the whole kingdom was riding on this.

*We're reworking the Bible, and we're looking to make it an all-time international best seller.   How would you like to be a part of that?* James, who considered himself a kind of a scholar, nodded slightly. The English offered another concession: *Not only that, we'll put your name on it!*

The final concession was about golfe.   *Look, H$^8$ picked up a lot of land in the 1500's, which he used for deer, cattle, pigs, sheep, and goats.   Since Elizabeth's time virginity and lighter meals came in, and this caused a severe cutback in livestock.   The land was now*

*James VI and I simplified the warning*

*mostly fallow. How would you as J¹ &⁶ like to bring your Scottish provincial games to the biggest part of the newly designated Great Britain?*

James went for it, adding the firstship of England to his sixthship of Scotland, bringing the game of golfe south. J⁶ and J¹ did a few more things for golfe. The *Bible* was another story. When he offered a few too many suggestions on *his* book, like, *Why do we say 'In the beginning God created the heaven and earth?' I think we ought to say, 'God, in the beginning, created heaven and earth.' It puts the subject first and the prepositional phrase second, or perhaps even better, the predicate could go second, and the prepositional phrase could go last. Yes!* The assorted scholars looked at one another.

J⁶ and J¹ went on- by God he liked this scholarly work. *And the next sentence starts with 'and' a conjunction! And look at all the sentences that start with conjunctions. That surely would get the Bible off to a bad start.* Aside: *(These English didn't seem to know the grammatical rules for their own language.)* With that a certain Dr. Andrewes responded that God used conjunctions to start sentences, and that they were just compiling God's words, not editing him. But the king would not relent. Finally, the scholars were about to explode when Sir Henry Savile, a learned layman, asked a seemingly unrelated question about golfe. *Why do you have such odd spellings?*

J⁶ and J¹ had never thought about it. Why is golfe spelled *golfe,* and whole, *whole,* clube, *clube? By Jove Sir Henry had a good point!* Golfe was an area where J⁶ and J¹ was sovereign. No arguments with an arbitrary God, or even worse, nit-picky scholars! So to make a long story short, James concentrated on golfe and let the scholars work directly with God on their version of *his book,* and golfe became golf, clubes became clubs, wholes became holes, *et cetera, et cetera, et cetera.*

Six months later reviewing a rough (pronounced ruff) draft of *his Bible,* and inspired by the simplicity of the language, J6 had another idea: He would change Macbeth's warning phrase to: *Watch before!*

# IV. The Scottish Enlightenment and Golf

The late 1600's and early 1700's marked the gradual anglicization of Scotland. In addition William (a Dutchman) and Mary as joint sovereigns replaced James II (of Great Britain), the last male Stuart to rule. Finally the two countries were essentially unified in 1707. This all had mixed results for Scotland. It had a bigger market and generally became more prosperous. Its feuds, battles, and wars declined. But also its distinctive culture and language started to be drowned in a sea of Englishness. All of this was to have an impact on golf.

*The rules caddy*

Politically some Scots tried to bring back the Stuarts, James, the "Auld Pretender" in 1715, and the dashing Charles (*Charlie is My Darling)* in 1745. These revolts ultimately failed.

So Scotland got even intellectually and artistically by producing some of the greatest thinkers, scientists, and businessmen in the world. This was called the "Scottish Enlightenment". It included men such as Frances Hutcheson, David Hume, Adam Smith. Robert Owen, James Watt, Robert and James Adam, Robert Burns, and Walter Scott.

By the mid to late 1700's golf had been under the influence of Knox for over 100 years. The rules had grown. There was a rule for almost every shot. There were rules for addressing the ball and for addressing one's fellow golfers. Of course the Scots being a canny and practical people did not memorize all these rules. They put them in a book- a multi-volume book. The volumes were so crucial, that they had to be taken on each round. This led to two things: much longer games, and the job of "rules caddie".

One of the leaders of the "Scottish Enlightenment" was Adam Smith. Smith was a moral philosopher and economist who tried to create a better life for ordinary people. He theorized about war and trade and religion. But he didn't stay in an ivory tower. He kept in touch with the real world by talking to ship owners and sailors, businessmen and laborers and others. When he observed golf, its voluminous rules, and the rule caddies, he suggested that it would be much better if its rules were simplified, and the book be kept centrally at a place like St. Andrews. When the rule caddies got word of this they marched on Edinburgh shouting something like, *It'll bae the runenation o' golf a' wae kno'it.* But their protests were overwhelmed by golfers, golfers' wives (or widows) and the 19th hole establishment.

*The rules caddies protested*

*Two poets from the Scotish Enlightment*

There were two others from the Scottish Enlightenment who have something to contribute to our story: Robert Burns and Walter Scott.

Robert Burns was born into a poor farming family. He had a great sense of freedom and dignity for the common man. He also liked to drink; he liked to wench, and liked folk songs. He wrote about all that, in words that are still memorable. Burns died at age 36. Walter Scott was a prolific writer, writing stories about Scottish history and legends, like *Rob Roy* and *The Lady of the Lake*.

They both speak to the modern golfer:

## On the golfer who might be tempted to cheat

*Oh, what a tangled web we weave,*
*When first we practice to deceive!*

*Lochinvar*
by Scott

## Planning for a perfect game and uncovering a mouse on the course

*But Mousie, thou art no thy lane,*
*In proving foresight may be vain:*
*The best-laid plans o' mice an' man*
                *Gang aft agley,*
*An lea'e us nought but grief an' pain*
                *For promis'd joy!*

*Still thou art blest compared wi' me!*
*The present only toucheth thee:*
*But och! I backward cast my e'e*
                *On prospects drear!*
*An' forward, tho' I canna see,*
                *I guess an' fear!*

*To a Mouse*
by Burns

## Trying to impress other golfers

*O wad some Power the giftie gie us*
*To see oursels as ithers see us!*

*To a Louse*
by Burns

---

## On making that one great shot

*Kings may be blest,*
*    but Tam was glorious*
*O'er the ills of life*
*    victorious*

*Tam O'Shanter*
by Burns

## Facing the next shot

*But pleasures are like poppies spread:,*
*You seize the flow'r its bloom is shed;*
*Or like the snaw falls in the river,*
*A moment white then melts forever;*

*Tam O'Shanter*
by Burns

## At the 19th hole

*Inspiring bold John Barleycorn!*
*What dangers thou canst make us*
*scorn!*

*Tam O'Shanter*
by Burns

## After 19th hole with wife at home:

*...We think na on the long Scots miles,*
*The mosses, water slaps and stiles,*
*That lie between us and our hame,*
*Where sits our sulky, sullen dame,*
*Gathering her brows like a gathering*
*storm,*
*Nursing her wrath to keep it warm.*

*Tam O'Shanter*
by Burns

---

## The perfect words to confront the wife with warm wrath

*O my luve's like a red, red rose,*
*That's newly sprung in June:*
*O my luve's like the melodie,*
*That's sweetly play'd in tune.*

*As fair art thou, my bonnie lass,*
*So deep in love am I,*
*And I will love thee, still my Dear,*
*Till a' the seas gang dry*

*A Red, Red Rose*
by Burns

# should auld acquaintance be forgot ♪

## Final Words

*Should auld acquaintance be forgot,*
*And never brought to mind?*
*Should auld acquaintance be forgot,*
*And days o' lang syne?*

*Auld Lang Syne*
by Burns

In many ways Burns and Scott tried to preserve part of auld Scotland. Golf, though, became a British game. This was to carry it around the world.

# V. The Witches Migrate: Golf and America

While the Scottish witches were proud o' their game, they didn't sit around resting on their caldrons. They took some seminars, for continuing education credits, updated their skill sets, and generally began *modernising*. One of things that they didn't want to do, however, was to lose their old skills. For golf that meant forecasting its future. They could see clearly through their eye of newt technique, that the biggest future market that they weren't in was America.

The witches were pretty full of themselves for having developed such a bewitching game. However, one day in sensitivity training, the leader-guru pointed out that maybe golf had been invented in America by the Hopewell Indians in the year 0 (Y0K in computerese). That would mean almost 1,000 years before the first shepherd hit the first rock into a hole, and his sheep dog retrieving it and telling all the other sheep dogs about it. He pointed out the evidence: hundreds of Hopewell mounds could be *golf bunkers*; also clubs and balls were found in the mounds. They seemed to only lack scorecards and golf moccasins, *but the search was continuing*.

This rocked the witches back on their heels. The leader-guru could see that they were upset (With his ponytail, beard, and sandals, he was above all, sensitive). He pointed out that the Hopewells didn't write it down. This was contrasted with the well-documented record of the Y1K tournament, even though its winner was unknown, the well-known Duncan-Macbeth rivalry, and other history tying golf to Scotland.

*The Hopewell Indians may have invented golf, but neglected to write it down*

The first written references to golf in America were in the late 1700's early 1800's in Charleston, South Carolina, and Savannah, Georgia. It is thought that the witches migrated to America with Scottish regiments of British troops. Scots and Scots-Irish fought on both sides of the American Revolution, especially in the South. It seemed natural that after the war, they would try to set up their own courses in the region. It is unclear what happened, but golf, if started in the American South, disappeared long before the Civil War.

*The leader-guru was above all "sensitive"*

One theory is that it suffered from "Mint Julep-Veran Dah"(MJVD) management. The theory goes like this: both Charleston and Savannah were well known for slave labor. Slaves laid out the courses creating the bunkers, tees, and greens. MJVD management oversaw everything and everything that they oversaw was good. Next came maintenance, cutting the grass, keeping the greens smooth, replacing divots. MJVD management also oversaw that, and that too was good. Finally came the playing; the slaves became the caddies.

The players found golf hard and frustrating. One golfer pointed out that the hole game violated their Mint Julep-Veran Dah style management. The slaves should be playing, and *they* should be overseeing. His arguments were cogent, and golf became a slave game.

Golf as a slave game worked well for a while. The owners created an MJVD Athletic Association (MJVDAA) which, in turn, developed tournaments for bragging rights and *friendly* wagers. Of course a person can be a lot friendlier about wagers if he wins. This desire to be friendly led to recruitment; recruitment led to rules therefor; and this led to violations. Owners might recruit before recruiting season; they might violate the rules during plantation visits; or worst of all, they might even pay some slaves *under the table* for success. The MJVDAA decided that that was unacceptable because it would *ruin the slaves' economic status.* After a lot of leaked stories by rival plantations, charges and counter-charges, and gnashing of teeth, the entire system broke down. Soon thereafter, budget cuts forced the closing of all the courses. The Mint Julep-Veran Dah style management went on to the next cause- secession, but all was not lost. Many of the MJVDAA rules were later adapted for college recruiting.

Meanwhile the witches developed a love for the new country, deciding that it had a lot of potential for using their talents. The South, though, was confining. Accordingly, they decided to migrate to other sections of the

*"Mint Julep-Veran Dah" (MJVD) Management*

*"Mint Julep-Veran Dah" Management at golf(e)*

country.  We have their words:

Witch 1:
*I will go to Washington*
*so full of noise and clamor,*
*I will convince the country*
*That it's a place of glamour.*

*For work I'l do a lobbyist be,*
*Tis just like prostitution,*
*And all the while I'll brag about*
*my love for Constitution!*

Impressive!  The other witches
could see (through their eyes of
newts) that Washington was a
perfect place for witches.  The
second witch spoke.

Witch 2
*For two careers, to New York I'l*
*go,*
*Advertising and PR will make it*
*so,*
*I'l lie and lie and lie and lie,*
*And as th'y say to the bank I'l cry.*

What better work could a witch
find?  It was the third witch's
turn.

Witch 3

*One witch flies to Washington to use*
*her skills as a lobbyist*

*Images the future will hold,*
*To Hollywood-to-be, I'l be bold,*
*Rape, murder, and depravity will screech,*
*When challenged I'l say freedom of speech!*

60

Thus the witches were to have great influence on America. But this gets us away from our main story on golf.

The first documented golf course in North America was established in Canada in the 1850's. It was thought to be brought by Scottish ships' officers. In 1873 the first golf club was established in Montreal.

In the United States in 1888, John Reid, a Scot-American had another Scot-American, Robert Lockhart, go to St. Andrews (to old Tom Morris's shop) to buy him a set of six clubs and some gutta percha balls. He then set up the first modern course of three holes in Yonkers, New York. On Washington's birthday he and some friends, sharing the clubs, played the first round recorded in the United States. Later they established a club as the St. Andrews Golf Society, which moved eventually to an apple orchard. The golfers became known as "The Apple Tree Gang".

Charles Blair Macdonald, a former student at St. Andrews, built the first 18 hole course in the Chicago area. He was favored to win the first open tournament in America at Newport, Rhode Island in 1894. He didn't. He questioned the legitimacy of the tournament, because it used stroke play rather than match

*Another witch flies to New York (New James) to work in advertising and PR*

*The third witch thought that Hollywood beckoned for her skills*

play. The next tournament was at St. Andrews in New York. Macdonald got to the finals of that, but then lost. He also questioned the legitimacy of that tournament because he was sore and ill. He officially became the first "sore loser", and the United States Golfers Association was formed. The next year Macdonald won at Newport and he declared the tournament, *a fine example of competition*.

Golf was gradually spreading when two other things happened. In 1898, Coburn Haskell of Cleveland, Ohio and Bertram Work, of B. F. Goodrich of Akron, Ohio invented a new livelier golf ball using tightly wound rubber threads. In 1900 the great Harry Vardon of (old) Jersey, made a U. S. tour under the sponsorship of A. G. Spaulding Co., an equipment manufacturer. In 1900, Vardon won the U. S. Open. He also demonstrated the famed Vardon grip.

*The Apple Tree Gang*

*Invention of new ball tightly wrapping rubber threads around rubber core*

In 1909, William Howard Taft became the first U. S. President-golfer. The 350-pound Taft was roundly criticized for it, but he helped focus the public's attention on the game. In 1913 Vardon returned to play in the American Open. He was defeated by a former caddie and store clerk, Francis Ouimet, who took a few hours off to enter the tournament. This democratized the game in America, just as the game had been democratized in Scotland centuries earlier. In 1922, another ex-caddie, and high school dropout, Walter Hagan, won the British Open. Finally the well-educated All American boy, Robert Tyre Jones, won the U. S. and British Opens and the U. S. and British Amateurs in 1930. The writer O. B. Keeler said of Jones, *Competitive golf is played mainly on a 5 1/2 inch course between the ears. This is where Jones excelled.* Jones retired at age 28 to build the perfect course at Augusta, Georgia with Scottish architect, Alistir Mackenzie.

Thereafter golfing became a popular pastime in America for more than 26 million people, five times the population of Scotland.

*William Howard Taft was roundly critcized for golfing as president*

*Bobby Jones wins U.S. and British Opens, U.S. and British Amatuers*

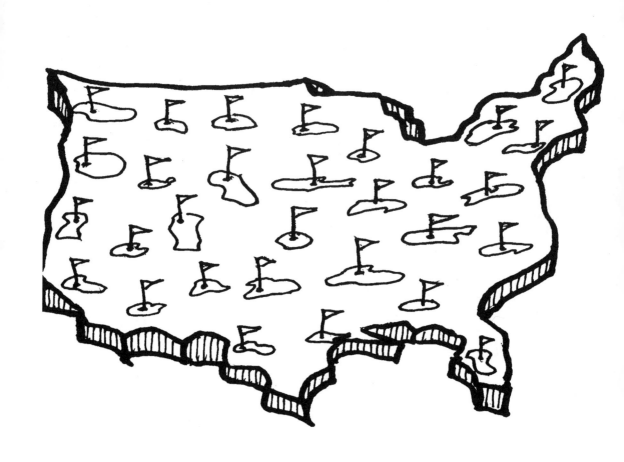

*Golf in the United States*

# VI Golf and the World; And Beyond!

We have seen the beginning of golfe in Scotland with the witches planning committee, shepherds and clubs, rocks, wholes, sheepdogs and fellow sheepdogs; the Y1K Tournament. We have seen the Duncan-Macbeth rivalry, and for the first time, in the context of golfe, may understand it. We have also seen the special contributions of Wallace and Bruce, five Jimmys in a row, John Knox and a Mary. Next we saw how James VI and I took golfe to England in the early 1600's, supervised *his Bible*, and simplified the spelling of golf.

The rest of the story is almost as dramatic: Soon thereafter golf spread to France and the other continental countries. Then it spread to the colonies around the world by British troops and businessmen from Australia, Borneo, Burma, Canada, and Ceylon, to Hong Kong, India, Jamaica, Kenya, to New Zealand, and Nigeria, Rhodesia, Uganda, and Zanzibar until it was said that, *the sun never sets on a game of golf.* After 1900 this was augmented by the in-

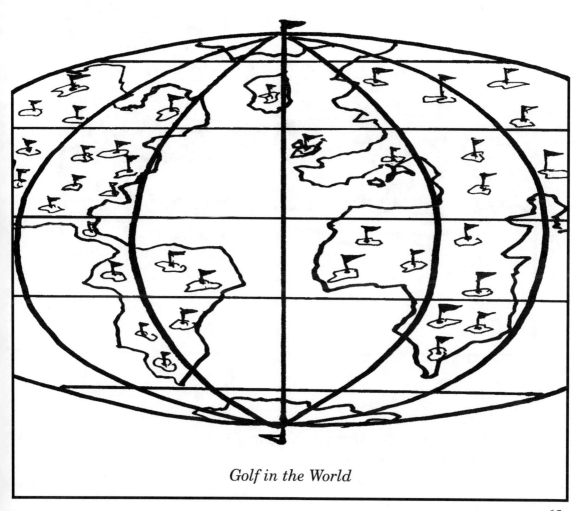

*Golf in the World*

creasingly ubiquitous American business men. The game today is so widespread that the 2000's may become known as the "Age of Golf". There are some notable adaptations to the game that began on the Scottish seashore.

In parts of Africa one is allowed to drop a ball without penalty if one hits a ball too close to a crocodile.

In the Sahara the traps are grass.

In Iceland golfers play with colored balls.

Hitler once played golf.  He cheated.

South of the equator a ball that circles in, tends to circle in counter-clockwise.  In Australia, if the ball lands in a kangaroo's pouch only the first jump counts.

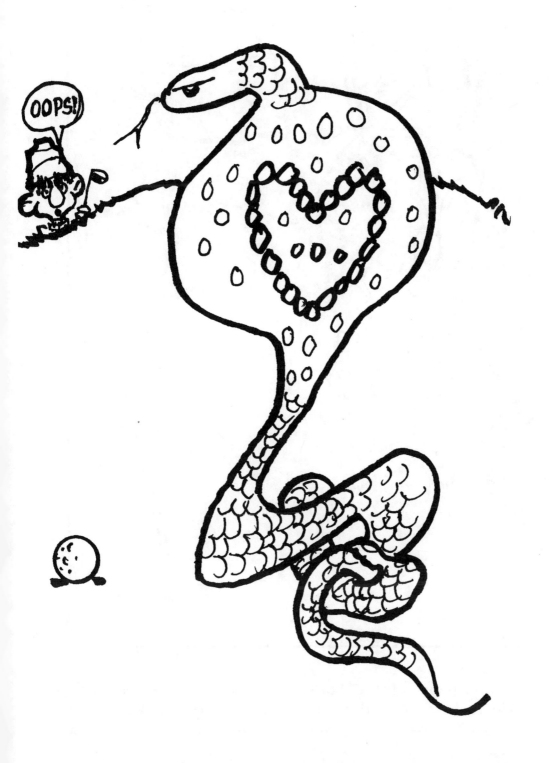

A hazard in India is the cobra.  They can cause a fatal lie.

In 1971 Alan Shepard hit a shot on the moon. It was described as *otherworldly*. He supposedly said. *One divot for mankind.* The official transcript was later changed to, *One divot for personkind.*[1]

---

1. There was a long argument whether the noun should be *personhood* or *personkind*. *Personkind* won out as being more reflective of his original words.

*This may be your day!*

**Now:**

Golf remains a bewitching game.  Take for example the following:

*It's a bright day; there are large puffy clouds against the brilliant blue sky.  The wind is gently rocking the trees, the birds are singing. You are off to your best game ever- a powerful straight drive, a subtle well-placed iron shot put you on in two, and the putt just caught the lip of the cup- a birdie three!  This may be your day!*

*You are beguiled as you walk to the next hole.  You know that you'll do the same thing.  You tee your ball up.  You scratch your ear, just like you did the last time.  You carefully line up the drive.  You notice in the sky how the clouds are slowly moving.  You listen to the birds and the gentle movement of the breeze.  It raises small ripples on the water hazard.  You even smell the grass; what a wonderful day to be alive! You carefully align your body.  You look at your driver.  You visualize what it will do- straight and far.  You lift your club for the swing remembering all those fundamentals-*

*Oops!*

# Postamble

**Author's Note:** Like many complex human endeavors, golf(e) did not develop out of thin air. In fact the air was generally thick, with one thing or another. Any way the point is that many things either affected or effected it, depending on personal preference. Some of those things are detailed below. These provide the serious amateur with more context for the genesis, and exodus, of golf(e).

# Chronology of Golf

## Scotland-To-Be

**Beginning:** Rocks, trees, sand, soil, highlands, lowlands, grass, gorse, heather, water, and other materials necessary created for golfe.

**A Few Days Later:** People

**Prehistory:** Stonehenge to the south. In future Scotland: Picts, Brits, Angles, and Germans wandering in from all sides. There goes the neighborhood!

**B. C.**

## Rome and Britain-To-Be

*In the beginning*

**55:** Julius Caesar invades Britain-to-be. Brings game *paganica* played with a feather stuffed ball. Caledonian witches observe. Caesar also acquires taste for pre-Angus beef, which will eventually lead to his downfall, literally.

**50:** Roman pasta makers complain to Roman Senate subcommittee about Caesar's imports of beef, ask for quotas. Caesar is out casting dice.

**44(Ides of March)** Caesar assassinated by senate subcommittee including Brutus.

**42:** Senate with pangs of guilt votes to name hottest month of the year for Caesar.

**25:** Augustus Caesar likes idea of months named after political leaders. Suggests that August would be a nice name for a month.

## World

**0(Y0K)** People confused by year 0. Argument begins whether first year starts from 0-1 or 1-2. "Zeroeese" and "Oneeese" develop fierce rivalry, form parties, and carry signs in public.

*People came to Pre-Scotland from all directions*

c. 0: Hopewell Indians build mysterious mounds.  Some believe they were the first golfe bunkers in America.  Hopewells neglect to write it down.

A. D.

*The Zeroese and Oneese got into violent debates*

**81**: Roman General Gnaeus Agricola conquers "Caledonia", pushes "Agricola culture" as alternative to continuous fighting.

**c. 122**: Roman leader Hadrian gives up on agricola culture policy, builds wall in southern Caledonia to keep Picts out of southern lands. Walls become hazard on early golfe courses.

*Around 500 A.D. at Camelot a young knight pulled a sword from a stone*

c. 500: An Irish tribe, the Scots, led by Fergus MacErc invade Caledonia. Give name to the land. Bring stone for later delivery to Scone. Later kings of Scots include Aidan the False and Eochaid the Venomous. Further south, a young knight-intern pulls a sword out of a stone. This sets a whole series of events in motion.

563: St. Columba lands at Iona. Begins conversion of tribes to Christianity. Fighting intensifies.

c. 800: Norseman discover Scotland, "a good place to fight".

## Scotland

843: Kenneth McAlpin unites Scots, Picts, Brits, and Norseman under government of Scotia. Sends stone to Scone.

Fall 998: Planning Committee, Scottish Witches Society meets on a heath in Scotland. Formulate new game called "golfe".

Late Summer 999: Bored shepherd hits rock toward rabbit hole. Bored sheepdog retrieves it.

Later Summer 999: Sheepdog confides in friends about new game. Soon bored shepherds all over Scotland are hitting rocks towards holes.

*Rabbit observing the first golf(e) shot*

**Height of Summer 1000**: Y1K Festival. First competitive golfe tournament. Too much liquid, fermented, corn consumed and results of tournament are unknown.

# England

**c. 1020**: King Canute's courtiers tell him that they are positive that he is divine.

**c. 1022**: King Canute says, *If I am so divine, I'll just reverse the flow of the tide.* Tide refuses to move. Courtiers go back to the drawing board.

*King Canute trying to reverse the tide*

**1034**: Duncan becomes king; organizes first foursome. Play by "Duncan rules". He shoots parsnip golf; Macbeth begins to seethe.

**1040**: Duncan meets with unfortunate "accident" at castle of key lieutenant, Macbeth.

**1040~later**: Dunsinane named "Designer Castle of the Year", mainly for its modern wall hangings. A new award for "Designer Castle of the Decade" announced. Lady Macbeth, now queen, becomes sanguine about Dunsinane's chances.

**1041**: Macbeth by royal decree issues new rules for golf. Also builds course next to castle to simplify commute and get early tee time.

**c. 1046**: Banquo dies mysteriously in ditch. First Banquoit announced. Banquo shows up! Macbeth shaken. Lady Macbeth remains sanguine.

*Social critics predicted that housing on golf courses would start a new trend*

**1050**: Dunsinane awarded "Designer Castle of the Decade". Social critics predict housing on golfe courses will start a new trend. A new award for "Designer Castle of the Century" announced. Lady Macbeth's sanguinity is beginning to show.

**c. 1056**: Birnham Woods is beginning to look a little shaky. Macbeth thinks the "rough" is growing. Lady Macbeth suffers from nervous exhaustion, seemingly worried that an unstable landscape will ruin the chances of Dunsinane being named "Designer Castle of the Century". Queen takes frog's blood potion (FBP) under doctor's orders . FBP doesn't work. The queen is dead. Macbeth thinks she should have died hereafter.

**c. 1057**: Birnham Woods Moves! Macbeth attacked, dies. Malcolm (III) becomes king. He marries Ingibjorg, relative of Thorfinn the Mighty. Golfe goes on.

**c. 1060**: While introducing herself, Ingibjorg chokes on her on name, dies.

*Birnham Woods heads for Dunsinane*

# England

**1066:** Edward the Confessor, confesses he doesn't want to be king anymore. Advises successor, Harold to find a compelling nickname. Too late! William of Normandy decides that he likes the name of William the Conqueror, defeats Harold (The Loser) at the Battle of Hastings. William becomes king.

*William the Conquer and Harold the Loser*

# Scotland

**c. 1070**: Malcolm III marries Margaret of Harold the Loser's family. English becomes official language of the Scottish government and golfe. Scottish profanity greatly enriched by Anglo-Saxon vocabulary. Margaret tries to stop it. Malcolm tells her that such language is necessary for golfe, and not to be such a saint.

**1093**: Donaldbane begins first of his two terms as king.

**1098**: Magnus Barelegs acquires western islands.

*Scottish profanity was enriched by Anglo-Saxonisms*

**c. 1100**: As tribute to Y1.1K, King Edgar lays cornerstone to Edgarburgh castle. Stone carver makes typo, castle becomes Edinburgh castle.

**1124**: David I, grandson of Malcolm III becomes king of Scotland, distributes large estates to Anglo-Norman favorites like de Brus and Balliol. Appoints friend Walter fitz Alan to top political job as high steward. High steward supervises lower stewards: ship, shop, and wine.

**1153**: David dies, is succeeded by Malcolm IV, (the Maiden).

**1165**: Malcolm, the Maiden dies, succeeded by William the Lion who negotiates Auld Alliance with France.

**1199**: Richard the Lion Hearted of the Plantangenet* family goes off to the crusades. Raises taxes to pay for it. Leaves his brother King John as ruler. John makes some bad appointments, including the Sheriff of Nottingham. An outlaw named Robin Hood flourishes.

*An outlaw named Robin Hood flourishes*

---

*The Plantagenet family received that name because the first Plantagenet wore an agenet plant in his hat.

**1215**: Barons complaining about tax forms, force King John to sign the *Magna Carta, i.e.* Great Chart, at Runnymede. It exempts all capital gains from taxation and extends filing dates. In an interview afterwords KJ says: *How oft the sight of means to do ill deeds, make ill deeds done!*

**1251**: Margaret becomes a saint. (See 1070).

**1272**: Edward I becomes king of England.

## England and Wales

**1285**: England conquers Wales. Welsh begin diabolical plan: name everybody Williams, Evans, or Jones. This confuses English.

*King John exempted capital gains*
*from taxes, and extended filing dates*

# England and Scotland

**1286**: Infant Margaret becomes queen. Dies on her way to Scotland. Edward I of England "recommends" John Balliol (the Empty Coat) as ruler. English begin playing Scottish golfe courses.

**c. 1290**: Edward's son "Little Eddie's" best friend makes suggestion on how to run kingdom. Edward I throws him out of tower "for demonstration purposes".

**1296**: Balliol starts "Golfe Rebellion". Defeated at Dunbar by Edward who takes Stone of Scone to England.

**1297**: William Wallace leads "Flasher Rebellion", defeats the English, under leadership of John de Warrene, at Sterling bridge.

*King Edward was rumored to have pushed a potential advisor out of the window for "demonstration purposes"*

**1298**: Edward I learns of defeat, throws a few advisors into the English Channel. Heads for Scotland. Defeats Wallace at Falkirk. Wallace heads for the Highlands.

**1305**: Wallace, betrayed, captured, and executed by the English. Robert de Brus (the Bruce) heads for Ireland. Gets idea for greens, and course maintenance, and starts arachnid watching.

**1307**: Bruce defeats English at Loudoun Hill. Edward has apoplexy. Before he dies, he asks Little Eddie to carry his bones at the head of his troops until Scotland is reconquered.

**1310**: Little Eddie drops Edward I's bones. Asks servants to reconnect the bones. Servants ask for "bone plan".

*The servants ask Little Eddie for a "bone plan"*

*The first 22 hole golf(e) course was*
*established at Bannockburn*

**1314**: English march north with Edward I's bones still unconnected. Bruce defeats them at Bannockburn. English lose 22 battle flags. Canny Scots replace parsnips with flags, thereby establishing 22 whole golfe course.

**1320**: Scottish Declaration of Independence at Arbroath sent to Pope.
**1321**: Scottish Declaration of Independence is misfiled under "Arbroath" by Vatican clerk.
**1323**: Vatican clerk's enemy, a Vatican auditor, finds Scottish Declaration and points out incompetence of clerk to Pope.
**1324**: Clerk filed to death. Pope signs off on Scottish independence.

*Vatican auditor finds the Scottish Declaration of Independence*

**1325:** Little Eddie turns bone plan over to servants. The bones are pretty dry by now. They begin reconnection, singing as they go along.

*The servants began to sing as they reconnected Edward's bones*

**1329**: The dying Bruce asks his friend James Douglas to take his heart on a crusade.  Initiates expression, *Have a heart*.

**1330**: James Douglas drops Bruce's heart in plain of Spain;  becomes disheartened, leans over to pick it up, slain by a heartless enemy.

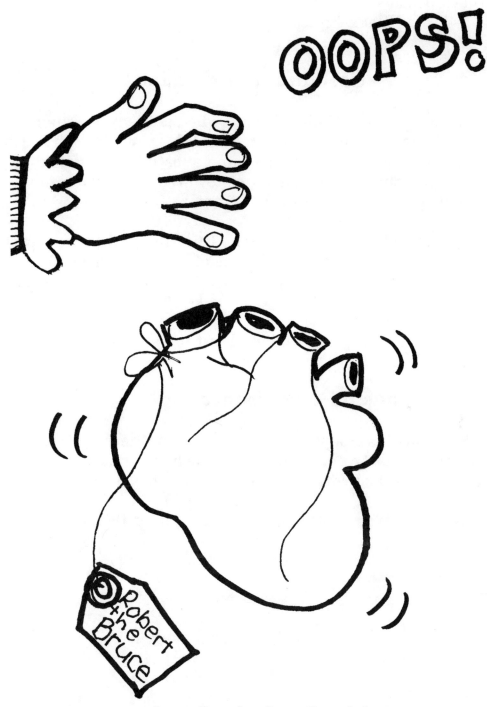

*James Douglas drops Bruce's heart*

# England and France

**1337**: The Hundred Years' War begins.

**1346**: English bowmen-yeomen defeat French knights in major upset at Crecy.

**1348-9**: Black death strikes Europe.

**1356**: Edward, the "Black Prince" wins great victory for English at Poitiers.

# Scotland and England

**1371**: Robert the Steward, "Auld Blearie" who married the daughter of Robert the Bruce, becomes Scottish king. To show common touch changes title to name, drops the "the", and substitutes "t" for "d" at end of name. The ship, shop, and wine stewards retain their jobs. Potential stewardesses remain in the wings.

**1394**: James I born.

**1406**: James sent to France to escape the English. Is captured by the English; King Robert dies when he learns of it. James, age 12, becomes a prisoner-guest of the English for the next 18 years. Is ransomed back to Scotland, vows to, *make the key keep the castle and the bracken bush the cow.*

**1412**: St. Andrews University founded. First intramural golfe programme established.

# England and France

**1415**: Henry V leads his troops into France with battlecry, *We few, we happy few, we band of brothers;* defeats French at Agincourt.

**1422**: Henry V calls the Scots "a cursed nation", dies, succeeded by Henry VI.

**1424**: James I returns to Scotland from a refreshing 18 year vacation in England.

**1428**: James I, renews Auld Alliance with France.

# England, Scotland, and France

**1429**: Henry VI and English besiege Orleans. Peasant girl, Joan of Arc, and Scottish troops save Orleans.
**1430**: Joan of Arc captured by the Burgundians, sold to the English.
**1431**: Joan of Arc executed.

*Joan of Arc and Scottish troops defeat the English*

# Scotland

**1437**: James I assassinated by friends and relatives without implementing the bracken bush policy. James II, "Fiery Face," age 6, takes over.

# England and France

**1453**: The Hundred Years' War ends in overtime. England loses land on continent.

**1455**: War of the Roses begins over "Who lost France?" The white roses of York initially win.

# Scotland

**1457**: Mashie invented. James II reacts by issuing decree, *that futeball and golfe be utterly cryit down and nocht usit...*
**1460**: Cannon blows up killing James II. Suspect flies away on broom. James III, age 9, becomes king.

*War of the Roses*

*King James II banned golf(e) and futeball*

# England

**1470**: The red roses of Lancaster come back for brief term.
**1471**: The white roses...

# Scotland

**1471**: James III renews ban on golfe.

*Richard III*

# England

**1483**: Richard III, wearing the white rose fights Henry of Lancaster wearing the red rose. Richard offers his kingdom for a horse; doesn't get it, is killed. Henry becomes Henry VII, the first of the Tudors.

# Scotland, Spain, and Pre-Columbian America

**1488**: James III faces rebellion led by Archie "Bell the Cat" Douglas. Falls off horse, and is reportedly killed by mashie. James IV, age 15, takes over.

**1491**: James IV issues decree fining and imprisoning those playing golfe.

**1492**: Columbus sent by Ferdinand and Isabella of Spain to "sail the ocean blue," looking for India, discovers America instead. Refuses to admit mistake, calls natives *Indians*.

*Columbus meeting natives*

# Scotland, England, France, and Spain

**1500**: Niblick invented to celebrate Y1.5K.

**1503**: James IV of Scotland, age 28, marries, Margaret Tudor, age 12, daughter of Henry VII of England in the famous marriage of the "thistle and the rose". The great age of Scottish poetry and music begins. He is also against golfe, but to see what he is against the Royal Treasury springs for a fewe clubes and balles. The balles stuffed with feathers are called "featheries".

**1509**: Henry VIII becomes king of England. His first words are: *Bring me a meal.* His second words are: *Bring me a woman.* He didn't have time for golfe. He marries brother's widow, Catherine of Aragon, daughter of Ferdinand and Isabella, but shows interest in castle intern, Anne Boleyn.

*Henry VIII shows interest in castle intern Anne Boleyn*

**1513**: To support the French, James IV leads splendid army to Flodden Field. Army loses. James reportedly is killed by a niblick. His body disappears. James V, age 17 months, takes over.

**1515?**: John Knox is born in Haddington, East Lothian, Scotland.

**1528**: Religious reformer Patrick Hamilton burned at the stake in St. Andrews. X marks the spot.

**1537**: James V is offered marriage by Henry VIII to his daughter, Mary, to Emperor Charles VII's sister, to Catherine de Medici by her uncle the Pope, and to Madeline, daughter of Francois I of France. He picks Madeline. In fit of excitement she dies.

**1538**: James marries Marie de Guise, also French. He travels around incognito, even caddies at golfe course, becomes known as "poor man's king".

**1542**: Mary to be Queen of Scots is born. Her father James V dies; he says, *It came with a lass,* (first royal Stewart married daughter of Robert the Bruce) *and will end with a lass.* Mary becomes queen while one week old.

*James V disguised as a caddy*

**1544**: Mary is pledged to marry Edward, prince of England, son of Henry VIII, and half brother to Elizabeth of England. Marriage deal repudiated by Mary's mother, Marie de Guise. England begins series of attacks on Scotland, *The Rough Wooing*.

**1546**: Religious reformer, George Wishart burned at the stake. Cardinal Beaton assassinated in retaliation.

## And Ireland

**1547**: Henry VIII dies. John Knox becomes a galley slave when captured by the French at St. Andrews. English create palisades in area of Ireland that they control. Area they don't control is *beyond the palisade*, or *beyond the pale* for short. English defeat Scots at Battle of Pinkie Cleugh.

*John Knox offened both Marys and Elizabeth*

**1548**: Mary sent to France with four other Marie's, and at age five, is betrothed to future French king, Francois, age four.

**1549**: John Knox released. Mashie niblick invented.

**1558**: Mary at 15, marries Francois who will become king of France. He claims English throne for wife as legitimate granddaughter of Henry VII. Elizabeth becomes disputed Queen of England. She follows motto, *Strike before being stricken.*

**1559**: John Knox returns to Scotland. Becomes leader of Scottish Protestantism which will be the official kirk (church) of Scotland. Begins formulating rules. Writes pamphlet aimed at two Mary's of Scotland: *The First Blast of the Trumpet against the Monstrous Regiment of Women.* Incidentally offends Elizabeth I of England.

**1560**: Mary's mother, Marie de Guise, dies in Scotland. Mary's first husband dies in France. Mary packs up to return to Scotland. Presbyterian church becomes the state church of Scotland. It issues its first book of discipline. Trouble brewing.

**1561**: Mary and Knox have conversation. It doesn't go well. She considers him insolent; he considers her frivolous.

**1565**: Mary, age 22, marries, her second cousin, Henry Stuart a.k.a. Lord Darnley, but seems intimate with Italian secretary and musician, David Riccio.

**1566**: Riccio murdered. Darnley is suspect. Mary flees with him to Dunbar. The future James VI and I is born.

**1567**: Darnley murdered. Mary plays golfe during his funeral. Bothwell is suspect for the murder. Mary marries Bothwell. Not a popular marriage. She is forced to abdicate in favor of her son, age 1, who becomes simply James VI, for the time being. Mary becomes prisoner in Scotland. Knox wins.

**1568**: Mary raises army, is defeated by army led by her half-brother, James Stewart, Earl of Moray. She flees to England. Fatal mistake; becomes prisoner-guest of her cousin Elizabeth I.

*Mary Queen of Scots golfing as her husband's funeral cortege passes by*

**1572**: Knox dies. Andrew Melville becomes Presbyterian leader. He devises system of separation of church and state.

**1586**: James VI, great grandson of Margaret Tudor, (marriage of thistle and rose) third cousin to Elizabeth, signs treaty with England. This ends the Auld Alliance with France.

**1587**: Mary, accused of plotting against Elizabeth, is tried, convicted, and executed.

**1588**: Spanish Armada defeated.

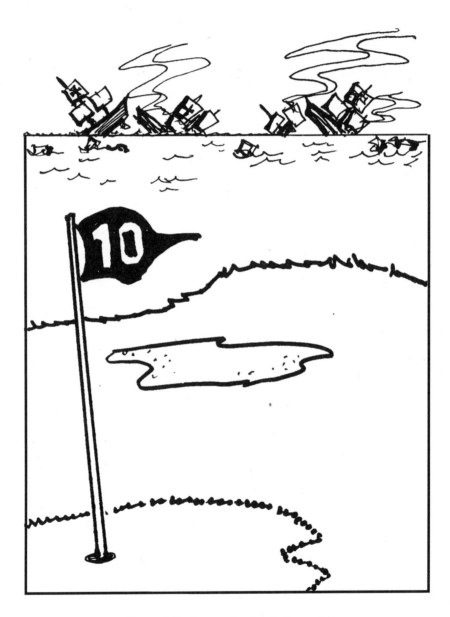

*Spanish Armada is defeated*

**1593**: Responding to "preacher pressure", Edinburgh Council bans golfe on Sundays.

**1593**: The following Sunday: Ban violated.

**1603**: Elizabeth dies; Scotland and England united under James VI and I. He takes golfe southe.

## And America

**1607**: First English colony founded in America. Colonists figure it can't hurt to call it James'town. Scribe drops apostrophe in water resulting in Jamestown. Country appears favorable for golfe. Emigration also encouraged to the northern part of Ireland.

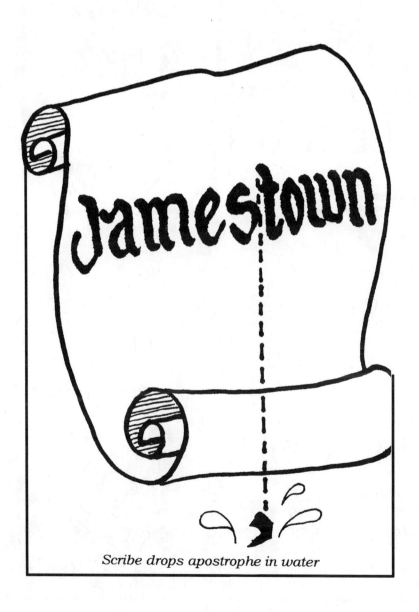

*Scribe drops apostrophe in water*

**1608**: James and Scottish buddies establish first English golfe course at Blackheath Commons.

**1611**: King James Version of The Bible issued. James modernises golf spelling.

**1620**: Pilgrims land at Plymouth Rock. *Mayflower* has no room for golf clubs.

**1625**: James I and VI dies, succeeded by son Charles I. Charles makes coronation speech about "the divine rights of kings." Not a hit.

*Charles I coronation speech on "the divine right of Kings" is not a hit*

**1628**: Petition of Right is drawn up by Parliament and presented to king. It limits king's rights to raise taxes without consent of Parliament, billet soldiers in private homes, the establishment of martial law, and illegal arrests.

**1638**: Charles wants to unite kingdom under Episcopalian religion, with "divine king". Scottish Presbyterians react by signing National Covenant.

**1641**: Charles tries to use his divine right in golf. Fails. Later golf game interrupted by news of the Irish Rebellion.

**1642**: Charles decides that Parliament is "getting uppity." Decides to arrest five members while they are in session. Parliament doesn't like it. English Civil War begins. Charles puts away his clubs.

**1644**: Combined Scottish army under Alexander Leslie and English army under Thomas Fairfax and Oliver Cromwell defeat king's army at Marston Moor.

**1646**: Charles surrenders to Scottish Coventeers. He is turned over to Parliament party in exchange for money and promise to make state church of England Presbyterian *i.e.* the Church of Scotland.

**1649**: The English aren't particularly keen on the Church of Scotland. Charles executed by Parliament.

**1653**: Oliver Cromwell becomes "Protector" of England, Scotland, Wales, and most of Ireland.

**1659**: After six years of Cromwell seriousness, the Stuarts are brought back. Charles II becomes king. Heads for clubhouse. His brother James becomes Admiral and Duke of York.

**1664**: Niew Nederland's name changed to New James to honor the king's brother. Clerk in hurry to meet with lady-in-waiting copies down title instead of name.

**1670**: Killing times begins in Scotland for those that don't go along with king. Scots begin diaspora.

**1678**: Charles's brother, the Duke of York and Johnne Patersone, Edinburgh shoemaker, defeat two Englishmen in golf for bragging rights in British Isles.

**1685**: Charles II dies, his brother, the Duke of York, becomes king, James II and VII.

*Ckerk in hurry to meet with lady-in-waiting
inadvertingly changed the name of New James*

**1688**: William(III), of Orange, a Dutchman, and Mary, daughter of James II replace James II of England, and VII of Scotland, the last of the male Stuart rulers, in the "Glorious Revolution". Most Scots take oath of loyalty except MacDonnells of Glengary and MacDonalds at Glencoe.

**1689**: Parliament passes the Bill of Rights, listing certain rights that were "true, ancient, and indubitable rights and liberties of the people".

**1690**: Battle of Boyne, near Derry or Londonderry. William III defeats army led by James II and VII. James escapes to France.

**1692**: With government encouragement, Campbells stage sneak attack on MacDonalds at Glencoe. This doesn't do much for William's image in Scotland.

**1694**: Mary(II) of William and Mary dies.

*Scots establish Bank of Scotland to support golf*

111

**1695**: Scots establish Bank of Scotland to support golf. Begin tradition of *In at ten, then out the door, on the links at least by four.* Scottish settle in Darien isthmus between North and South America as trading post.

**1699**: Darien settlement failing, appeals to William for help. William turns them down. This further embitters Scots against William.

**1701**: James, formerly II and VII dies in France. His son aspires to be James III and VIII.

**1703**: William dies. Mary's sister becomes Queen Anne. Queen Anne designs furniture and grows wild carrots. Later gets own war with France.

*Queen Anne agreeing with herself*

**1707**: Anne representing England, Scotland, and Wales formally agrees with herself to Act of Union merging countries into Great Britain. Scots granted free trading rights.

**1714**: Queen Anne dies without survivors. Crown again in dispute. English favor George I, a German, and grandson of James VI and I's daughter. Others prefer, Anne's brother as James III and VIII, who becomes "the king over the water".

**1715**: James III and VIII decides to strike. His agent, Lord Mar (Bobbing John) raises the auld Scottish standard at Braemar, and proclaims James the new king. Symbolically the golden ball at the top of the flagpole falls to the ground, thus "marring" the event. About 12,000 clansmen, called Jacobites, join them and they capture Perth. The Jacobites lose at Preston, and fight a standoff near Dunblaine. James lands, telling his followers, *For me it is no new thing to be unfortunate, since my whole life from the cradle has been unfortunate.* This fails to inspire and James and Lord Mar are forced to escape to France. The government cracks down on Scottish language and culture.

*Lord Mar at Braemar*

**1723**: Adam Smith born at Kirkaldy, Fife, Scotland.  Copper club invented, the "coppery".

**1724**: The coppery fails during rainstorm.

**1727**: The German speaking George I dies, replaced by the German speaking George II.

**1729**: Black Watch regiment founded to watch for blackguards in Scotland.  When not watching they play golf.

*The Black Watch regiment golfing when*
*they weren't watching for blackguards*

**1744:** Honourable Company of Edinburgh Golfers founded. Sponsors first competition in modern golf. Won by surgeon, John Rattay, who establishes link between doctors and golfe.

*First golf competition winner, Dr. John Rattay,*
*establishes link between golf and medicine*

**1745**: Bonnie Prince Charlie, son of James III and VIII, the auld pretender, invades Scotland, raising the Stuart banner again. Many highlanders join him on his march to Edinburgh. He meets government forces at Prestonpans and defeats them. He heads south reaching Derby (pronounced Darby), 130 miles from London. His advisors counsel him to withdraw and reorganize. Withdraws to Inverness in Scotland.

*Bonnie Prince Charles leading the
Rebellion of 1745*

**1746**: Government troops under the king's son, William Augustus, the Duke of Cumberland, meet Charles' troops at Culloden Moor. Jacobites routed. With the help of Flora MacDonald, Charles escapes to Isle of Skye dressed as a woman. Arms, kilts, tartan plaids, and bagpipes forbidden by the government.

*Bonnie Prince Charlie left for Skye*
*dressed as a woman*

**1754**: Ancient Club established at St. Andrews.

**1759**: Robert Burns is born at Alloway in Ayrshire. Adam Smith publishes his *Theory on Moral Sentiments*. James Wolfe defeats the French in Canada. Zinc club invented, the "zincie."

**1760**: The zincie fails in live tests. George II dies. His grandson, George III, the stamp collector, begins his 60 year reign.

**1764**: The standard of 18 holes is established for golf.

**1766**: James, the "auld pretender" dies. Charles, the "young pretender" becomes "the king over the water".

**1769**: James Watt, of Glasgow University, receives patent for improved steam engine.

**1771**: Walter Scott is born. Elements of copper club and zinc club combined to form "brassie". Pay dirt!

**1776**: American Revolution; Adam Smith publishes *Wealth of Nations*.

**1780**: As a reward for *Wealth of Nations,* Smith becomes Commissioner of Customs in Scotland.

**1786**: Burns publishes his first volume of poetry and songs.

**1788**: Burns becomes a customs worker for the government. Charles, the young pretender dies.

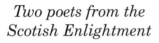
*Two poets from the Scotish Enlightment*

**1789**: The French Revolution begins, becoming a major issue in Great Britain and America. George Washington becomes first president of the United States.
**1790**: Adam Smith dies.
**1791**: Burns publishes *Tam O'Shanter*.

*George Washington becomes the first president of the United States*

**1792**: Burns promoted to Dumfries Port Division.

**1793**: King Louis XVI and Marie Antoinette executed in France.

**1795**: First evidence of golf in South Carolina.

**1796**: Burns dies.

**1800**: Act of Union joins Ireland to Great Britain.

**1811**: First evidence of golf in Savannah, Georgia.

**1812**: Napoleon invades Russia with *Grande Amree* of 600,000 troops; discovers burned out Moscow; retreats, *Armee* ceases to be *Grande*.

**1815**: Napoleon loses at Waterloo.

**1834**: The Royal and Ancient Club at St. Andrews receives a Royal Charter.

*Napoleon's retreat from Moscow*

**1837**: Queen Victoria begins her long reign.

**1848**: A statue of Hindu god *Vishnu* shipped from Asia to Scotland to Rev. Dr. Robert Patterson. It is wrapped in gutta percha, a rubbery material. His son suggests that it is an ideal material for golf balls, replacing the expensive and sometimes fragile featheries. New ball called guttie. Golf becomes much cheaper. Stroke play becomes common.

**1850**: Golf comes to Canada.

*Gutta percha used as packing material for statue*
*of Vishnu sent to Rev. Dr. Patterson*

**1860**: First British Open-to-All tournament held. Won by Willie Park of Scotland. He capitalizes on his fame by writing a book on golf.

**1861~1867**: Old Tom Morris wins four British Open championships. He sets up pro-shop in St. Andrews.

**1868~1870**: Young Tom Morris, a teenager, wins three British Open championships. Wins championship belt permanently.

**1870**: Golf bag invented by caddie tired of dropping clubs.

*Caddy decides a golf bag would be a good idea*

**1871**: No British Open championship while Scots search for new prize. Come up with claret jug.

**1872**: Young Tom wins again.

**1873**: Royal Montreal Club founded. First permanent club in North America.

**1875**: Young Tom, age 24, dies suddenly. Buried at St. Andrews.

**1888**: John Reid, a Scotsman, organizes St. Andrews Club, Yonkers, New York, first successful club in the U. S. First foursome includes two women.

**1890**: John Ball becomes first Englishman to win a British Open.

**1890's**: Brits, Harry Vardon, James Braid, and J. H. Taylor become first professional golfers.

*The first successful golf club in the U.S.*

**1893**: Charles Blair Macdonald builds first 18 hole course in the U. S. at Belmont, Illinois.

**1894**: First U. S. Open at Newport, RI. Macdonald favored; loses. Questions legitimacy of tournament. St. Andrews Club in New York announces match play tournament. Macdonald gets to final and loses. Macdonald questions the legitimacy of tournament becomes first "sore loser". USGA formed.

**1895**: USGA sponsors tournament at Newport. Macdonald wins. Declares tournament, *a fine example of competition*.

**1898**: Coburn Haskell of Cleveland, and Bertram Work of B. F. Goodrich Company in Akron, invent new ball tightly wrapping rubber threads around rubber core. Considered too lively to control by many.

**1900**: Harry Vardon, preeminent British golfer from (old) Jersey, makes first tour of U. S. as promotion for A. G. Spalding Co. Shows Americans famous Vardon grip. Wins U. S. Open.

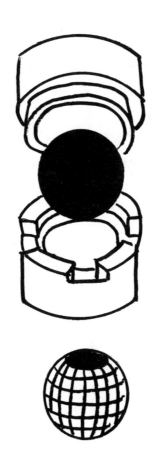

*Invention of new ball tightly
wrapping rubber threads around rubber core*

**1901**: Australian American, Walter J. Travis wins U. S. Open with Haskell ball. Guttie finished.

**1904**: Travis wins British Amateur, first non-Brit to win.

**1908**: William Taylor adds dimple effect to balls by reversing molds.

**1909**: William Howard Taft becomes first golfing U. S. President. He is roundly criticized for it.

**1913**: Harry Vardon returns to play in U. S. Open. Loses grip. Defeated in playoff by unknown American, Francis Ouimet, at Brookline, MA.

*William Howard Taft was roundly critized for golfing as president*

**1914**: Great War begins.

**1915**: Golf ball standardized to 1.62 inches diameter, 1.62 ounces in the United States.

**1916**: PGA is organized. First PGA Tournament held. Won by James M. Barnes.

**1920**: Golf tee invented by dentist, William Lowell, approved. In an emergency it can be used as a toothpick.

**1921**: Warren G. Harding becomes golfing president for which he is roundly criticized.

**1922**: American high school dropout, Walter Hagan, wins British Open.

*Golf tee was invented by dentist, William Lowell, and can be used as a toothpick in an emergency*

**1926:** First steel shafted clubs authorized in U. S.

**1929:** St. Andrews authorizes steel shafted clubs.

**1930:** Bobby Jones wins U. S. and British Opens, U. S. and British Amateurs. Retires at age 28 to build perfect course at Augusta with Scotsman, Alistir Mackenzie.

**1931:** Concave Texas sand wedge banned.

**1932:** The United States officially adopts a golf ball 1.68 inches in diameter. St. Andrews favors ball no larger than 1.68 inches, but permits smaller European ball. In Europe Americans can use either ball. In America Europeans must use American ball. Gene Sarazen (Eugenio Saraceni) wins U.S. and British Opens using straight-faced sand wedge.

**1933:** Straight-faced sand wedge not banned. Johnny Goodman last amateur to win U. S. Open.

**1934:** Horton Smith wins first Masters tournament.

**1935:** Gene Sarazen's double eagle at The Masters helps him win.

**1936:** Patty Berg wins first U. S. Women's Open.

**1938:** Sam Snead becomes leading money winner.

**1940:** Jimmy Demaret, a nightclub singer, wins first of his three Masters.

**1945:** Byron Nelson wins eleven straight events.

*Jimmy Demaret singing and winning*

**1947**: Babe Didrikson Zaharias becomes first American woman to win British Ladies Championship.
**1949**: Ladies Professional Golf Association formed.

*Babe Didrikson Zaharias, an all around athlete, was the first American woman to win the British Ladies Championship*

**1951:** Ben Hogan wins second U. S. Open in a row after nearly being killed in auto accident.

**1953:** First nationally televised golf tournament held at Tam O'Shanter in Illinois. Dwight Eisenhower becomes golfing President for which he is roundly criticized.

*Dwight Eisenhower becomes golfing President, for which he is roundly critized*

**1955**: Arnold Palmer wins his first professional tournament.

**1958**: Palmer wins first of four Masters Tournaments.

**1962**: Arnold Palmer says, *I wish I was playing anybody, but that big strong, happy dude.* Big, strong, happy dude, Jack Nicklaus, defeats Palmer in playoff for U. S. Open.

**1963**: Mickey Wright wins thirteen events on female tour.

**1971**: American Astronaut, Allan Shepard plays golf on the moon. Has astronomical experience. *One divot for mankind.* Lee Trevino wins U. S., Canadian, and British Opens.

**1974**: St. Andrews adopts the larger American ball for the British Open.

One divot for ~~mankind~~
personkind

**1975**: Johnny Miller wins eight tournaments.

**1977**: Tom Watson defeats Nicklaus in the Masters and the British Open.

**1978**: Nancy Lopez wins five tournaments in a row.

**1983**: Tom Watson wins his fifth British Open title.

**1985**: Kathy Whitworth wins 88th title.

**1986**: Nicklaus wins his sixth Masters.

**1988**: China opens Arnold Palmer designed course. Refuses to give visas to "Arnies Army".

*China opens Arnold Palmer designed course*

**1997**: Tiger Woods wins Masters at age 21.
**1999**: The Scots elect their own Parliament for the first time since 1707.
**2000**: Golf continues...

*The Scots elect their own Parliament after 292 year interruption*

# Appendix 1

## Sources of Quotes and Paraphrases Used in the Book

# In review...

# INDEX

**James B. Cash** for some reason was born in a railroad hospital in Chicago, Illinois. He grew up in East Chicago, Indiana, where he was a fairly unsuccessful class clown. He attended DePauw University in Greencastle, Indiana, and St. Andrews University in St. Andrews, Scotland. He didn't play golf(e) there. He came home; worked for the government; worked for business, where he literally had the good fortune to have his retirement funds surge upward in the Great Bull Market. This enabled him to write for a living. Now he needs to sell books. He is married to Nancy (Neely) Cash. They have a son, James Aaron, and three daughters, Stephanie, Diana, and Jennifer.

**Walt Kaye** has been drawing cartoons for publication since he was in Latimer Jr. High School in Pittsburgh , Pa. in 1950. He served in the U.S. Navy and the U.S. Air Force, working as an illustrator.
He attended the University of Dayton and the Dayton Art Institute School, studying Advertising Design. In 1962 he began working as a graphic designer at NCR Corporation. Walt retired from NCR in 1994 as a manager of a computer graphic department. After retirement he became a full time caricature artist.
In 1960 Walt married Kay Squires, who then became Kay Kaye. They have three grown daughters, Colette, Karen, and Marcella.
In 1991 Walt had a life saving liver transplant, so he is very active in organizations promoting organ donation. He draws many crowds at health fairs, hospitals, churches, and schools.